Dearheart: Poems From a Centenarian Woman at Summerford

Mayo Hindle

Published by AllrOneof Us Publishing, 2020.

While every precaution has been taken in the preparation of this book, the publisher assumes no responsibility for errors or omissions, or for damages resulting from the use of the information contained herein.

DEARHEART: POEMS FROM A CENTENARIAN WOMAN AT SUMMERFORD

First edition. October 9, 2020.

Copyright © 2020 Mayo Hindle.

ISBN: 979-8201028756

Written by Mayo Hindle.

To those who loved Mayo: Will Hindle, Jude Johnston and many others.

"If my writings bring a smile or a tear

I will thank my God for having been here,

And pray my thoughts came from heaven above,

Given to you, written in love."

Mayo

INTRODUCTION

MAYO HINDLE, BORN IN the 19th century, wrote most of these poems in her mid-nineties, and went on to live to 103. She resided in a nursing home in the deep South, having outlived her son, who died near the time that many of these poems were written. Will Hindle was a well-known independent filmmaker, who won many awards with films such as *Chinese Fire Drill* and *Watersmith*. I had the good fortune of attending a week-long, film making workshop and came to know Will and his work. I did not meet his mother, however, who ended up in a nursing home in Falkville, Alabama. There, a friend of mine, Brother Jude, would visit her regularly.

One day, many years ago, Jude gave me this manuscript, thinking I might be able to do something with it. At the time, her poems seemed remote from the work I had done, publishing oral histories of persons who had been homeless or in psychiatric hospitals. But I recently chanced across the manuscript again and thought it was time to honor this woman.

Mayo, who I came to know as I edited this volume, is a testament to being a loving person and one who received love. Her writing is homespun, deceptively simple and tinged with humor. Her voice is the wisdom of age speaking to us, one who has been through much, and who conveys sayings that can serve as a valuable guide to life. As an expert in aging, she can advise how to "keep the spirit of youth, that as we come to look more like a prune, to be like a peach inside. In one of her poems, which speaks to me and is titled "Wouldn't it be Wonderful," she offers a worldview that looks for the good in things.

> *Wouldn't life be worth living*
> *If we praise the good we see?*

Spirituality informed her life, and her faith was true and simple, one that graced her life and made her a more loving person. At least that is the testament of Brother Jude who wrote when I announced my intention to publish her work: "She was a true child of God in my estimation."

Mayo's life was a testament to how beauty, creativity, and love can be present at all times in our life, even our "twilight" years. It's also a testament that this beauty can be present no matter where we are, even a nursing home. Somehow love and the spirit mesh together, emblematic in her son's creative journey in the world, and his heartfelt love that is expressed in his letter published here as the Afterword.

Last, I mention *Dearheart*, which became the title for this work. As I was editing Mayo's work, I, at first, thought it was a mistake. The manuscript was printed by an old portable typewriter and had such errors present. But the newly coined word repeated, and it appeared to be a reference to a special friend of Mayo. We may not think of Nursing Homes as being a place where a rich love could be present. But Mayo tells us so, where her love for many of the patients and staff at Summerford abounded, as with her friend, "Dearheart."

So, as I conclude this, I have come to see that Mayo was one of God's unknown Saints, and I have had the honor of sharing this work.

Michael A. Susko,

Editor

WOULDN'T IT BE WONDERFUL?

Wouldn't this old world be better
If the ones we meet would say.
I know something good about you
And then would treat us that way.

Wouldn't life be a lot happier
If the good that's in us all
Was the only thing about us
That they bothered to recall?

Wouldn't life be worth living
If we praise the good we see?
For there's a lot of goodness
In the worst of you and me.

Wouldn't it be nice to practice
That fine way of thinking, too
You know something good about me,
I know something good about you.

IF THEY ONLY HAD LOVE

Oh the beauty of this city
With its hills and shining bay.
If the dear old ones we pity
Could just walk along this way
But so many, are forgotten
Left alone, in lonely rooms,
Who am I to know about them ? ?
'Cause I too, live in these tombs.

God is good to those who thank him
For their daily bread and rest,
But we too, must do our duty
When he puts us to the test,
We are *still here* for a reason
Not to wish for end of life,
Use your strength, be up and doing
And you'll find there's little strife.

Every morning God will give us
A new day to do our best,
Thank him for the night of silence
Thank him for the peace and rest.
Now's the time to meet the others

Get them out their lonely room
"Howdy neighbor," let's get going
And disperse this world of gloom.

Yes, we're lonely for our loved ones
But we're independent now,
Take advantage of our freedom
And let's make a solemn vow
To be cheerful and love others
In this world of grief and woe
Don't be sorry, God will answer
When it's time for us to go.

Written in San Francisco, California
Nineteen seventy-two.

RARE OLD ROOMMATES

I learned patience from "Little Annie King"
I love her more than anything...

LIVE AND LEARN

YEARS AGO IN BUSINESS I strove to
    Do more, to have more and to be somebody.
    Years have passed remembering that desire
    For better worldly living.

    I now know I was hungry to be free from
    Inferiority and other shortcomings.
    So instead of wanting to have more
    And to be somebody, I now know

    I already have more, I am already somebody
    (a child of God) with *perhaps*
    One talent and free to express it now.

THINGS I HAVE

(OUT MY WINDOW)

I HAVE A GOOD HOME in which to reside
   I'm cozy and warm when it's cold outside.
   See fountains and flags waving in the breeze
   Beautiful flowers and the tall pine trees.
   Visitors pass by and wave to me
   That makes me happy as can be.
   Cool in the summer, birds in the spring,
   I guess I *have* about everything.
   I look to the heavens where angels trod,
   But most of all, I *have God*.

FRIENDS OR JUST COMPANY?

THROUGH SICKNESS OR health, we learn.
    We all know persons whom we call friends.
    But whose friendship is so fragile
    As to stand almost no strain without breaking.
    And there are friends (only a few)
    Whose friendship has been tested through long
    Experiences and would be next to impossible to destroy.
    There's a great difference having company
    And having a friend. company must be entertained
    While your friend may sit in silence, but you
    Know they are there. "complete trust needs no words"

ME IS THINKING NINETEEN SEVENTY THREE

What would I do without my friend,
Who listens to my silly odes, without end?
I think, I scribble the thoughts in my mind,
I phone her, she listens and then she will find
Something of interest that I should keep on,
So I struggle to please, then my mind is gone.

Not a thought comes to me, so I sit down and ponder,
Poor little me, is it any wonder
That I'm losing my mind, a little each day?
It would be different, if I got any pay.
but
I don't so I
quit.
from the desk of the president?

To the members on the first meeting.
Remember this:

> We are "young and *wise,*
> Not old and foolish."

They asked us to form a committee
To tell if we have any doubt
Be it good or bad, whatever we had,
To speak up and "shout it out"

We'll find help comes "on the double"
They try *always* to be fair,
To untie the "knots" in our trouble
That shows they *really do care*

Be alert, attend every meeting
Never mind the rain or sprinkles,
We all have *three* things in common,
Life, gray hair and *wrinkles.*

Signed Mayo (voted Pres.?)
(What a laugh)

Here's to our good health and comfort,
And a little fun, too.
Know any good stories???

There may be a time
When these "slips" of mine
Come out in repetition.
Don't blame the machine,
You know what I mean,
The "brain" is out of commission.

THE RIGHT WILL
WIN

THIS IS WHAT I TRULY believe, that what I need, I will receive,
  I'll put my problem into God's hand,
  That way I won't *have to* understand.

  tears or laughter, pleasure or pain
  I'll not falter in speaking up again
  To those who *won't* listen or even believe
  That what I need, I *will* receive.

  The more I love, the more I find
  That life is good and friends are kind.
  So why should I worry, why should I fret?
  For what they are *giving* is what they will *get*.

LIFE'S LIKE THAT

I know I'll have some bad days,
I know I'll get some rain,
But I know, too, it doesn't help
To get angry and complain.

But I *dooded* it anyway
I phoned straight to the "head"
They came, sat down and listened,
And this is what I said.

Come what may, I can't change that,
But while I live today
I demand respect and privacy
In a more *modest* way.

(in the bath)

JUST ONE OF THOSE DAYS

I tell you, little Ann
It's a pain and a hurt,
The old body's going down
While the brain's still alert.

At night my thoughts go round and round
Thinking of things to do,
Like reading and writing or cleaning my room
Or even writing "ditties" to you.

Each night on my knees
By the side of my bed
I pray strength for the body
And ease the pain in my head.

Each day brings me closer to "home."

I have lived from the nineties in the nineteenth century
Into the eighties of the twentieth century.

The old year is gone, so I walk by faith
Into another year.

The best of life is always farther on.

When you have a sudden setback, part of your life is gone,
But another part comes up.

Have eyes not only to see, but to look after,
Have ears not only to hear, but to listen to,
Minds to understand, hearts to touch and hands to give.

A FATHER'S PRAYER

I read a poem, so well done,
From a father to his son.

"In my heart I'll plant a seed,
That of a flower, not a weed
Soon a son for all to see
Will be the man I hope he'll be

Don't waste time seeking "thrills"
Smoking pot or popping pills.
God will help you and give you health,
Love and confidence, not necessary wealth.

Now he's a man for all to see,
He is the man I prayed he'd be
Father, for all you've said and done,
You're a *great dad,* yes, you're the one.

ANGIE, WAS THAT YOU?

In the night I was hungry,
An angel brought cookies and milk,
I reached up and touched her hair
To me, it felt like silk.

So it *must* have been an angel
It was dark, I couldn't see,
So all that I remember is
How sweet she was to me.

JESUS

"J" is the *joy* he brings us
"E" we can *excel* if we try,
"S" oh how he must have *suffered*
"U" for the *universe* and sky
"S" we ask, is he truly *satisfied*
With the work we are trying to do?
Bless us, dear Jesus, our savior,
we love and trust only you.

I can't compete with your alphabet,
I hope you understand
with this "ingenious"? mind
I'll do the best I can.

"A" is for apple, "B" is for ball
"C" is for cat, "D" southern drawl,
"E" is for evil, "F" is for fear,
Sorry, brother Talley
I'll have to stop here.

EGO

Some days I am very proud,
Think things are just fine.
I worked *hard* for what I have
And they are really *mine*.
I am a self-made man,
Think only of tomorrow,
I didn't give a helping hand
For I *neither lend* nor *borrow*.

One day I picked up a *bible*.
Found I could get "help" in my fight.
So I breathed *out ego*, breathed *in God*.
It turns out, "The bible is right."

A PIPE DREAM

Tell me, should I give up,
'Cause my body's slowing down?
I have enthusiasm, so
I think I'll "go to town"

If I had a bicycle
And if I knew the way,
I'd go to one of Walmart stores,
And spend the whole darn day.

See all the *wonderful* bargains,
Things I'd like to buy,
But I have no money
So there's no need to try.

Come back home and think of
The *gorgeous* things out there.
All tired out, kick off my shoes
And *flop* in my easy chair.

I'll say it's a pipe dream,
I woke up to find,
That all my day's activities
Were only in my mind.
poor ol' soul, Mayo

Pity? No, laugh? Yes.

SOON ANOTHER BIRTHDAY
How fast the years roll by,
I find that more the years,
The easier it is to try.
I can't put on canvas the scenes I behold
They can't be framed in silver or gold.
I must have sights, I must have sound
I get them only, from the sky to the ground.
I try to have reason for why, when and where,
We know *who* is, he's always here.
So let me frame, not in silver or gold
But in the window of my soul.

HE IS IN MY HEART, I always find
Every poem I write he puts in my mind,
So if you like them give God the praise
I'll write what he dictates the rest of my days

TO MY GOOD FELLOWS

THERE MAY BE DAYS WHEN you're sad and blue,
　　But how that day goes is up to you.
　　Think back, when it was "early to rise"
　　Before the sun rose in the skies.
　　Setting your loved ones to school and work,
　　You stay home to do work you can't shirk.
　　Now they're all grown and are gone,
　　So now your work on earth is done.
　　Old and painful, you say "it's not fair"
　　But that's the "cross" we all must bear.
　　"The Summerford home" of *loving care*
　　Is the "waiting room" to our "home" up there
　　So ignore the pain, enjoy the pleasure,
　　They *really could* call us,
　　"ladies of leisure."

ME

ONE is a lonely number
  If only someone would phone,
  No thoughts, no rest, no slumber, „
  So tired of being alone.

  then

I counted my many blessings
More than I'd ever known,
I closed my eyes and *talked* to him.
He tells me, "I'm not alone"
It's not that I'm indolent,
It's not that I'm lazy
By not coming out
Looking fresh as a daisy.
I'm getting older one day at a time,
The strength I once had
Is no longer mine.
When asked, "how I am"
I say, "fine" (with a grin)
It's better than telling
The shape that I'm in.

COME & GO

COME, all of you who are weary,
　　Listen, what God has to say
　　About his son, Christ Jesus,
　　Start being *a worker today.*
　　Go, talk to some unsaved one,
　　Tell of many blessings you receive,
　　All God asks us to do is
　　Trust and *obey* and *believe.*
　　How wonderful to know he is risen
　　And living in our hearts today,
　　"Bless us," dear Jesus, our savior,
　　Shower us with love *when* we pray.

BLESSINGS

OLD WIVES TALES SAY, "when you have twins"
 That's when old *double trouble* begins,
 Now we well know that is not true,
 They're double "blessings" sent to you.
 God knows why he sent them from up *there*
 To parents who will raise them in loving care.
 So thank the Lord for these "bundles of love"
 He sent them to *you* from heaven above,
 How fortunate to have "grandma" to fill in the gap
 How delightful to see kids fight for her lap.

HELP

DEAR LORD, HELP ME write my confessions,
   This world is no longer mine
   I have no earthly possessions
   All I have is your precious time.
   You say, "ask" and we shall be given
   You say, "seek" and we shall find,
   You say, "knock" and the "door" will be opened
   Oh Lord, forever be mine.
   I will try to keep your commandments
   Do unto others, as you say,
   I now place my commitment,
   And will *never* forget to pray.

   Amen.

IS IT TOO LATE?

I LIE IN MY BED AND think of the past
    How sad it seems somehow,
    To think of the things I *should* have done,
    But it's too late to turn back now.
    I *should* have read my bible more,
    And taught the young ones how,
    Oh, there's so much I *should* have done
    But it's too late to turn back now.
    For the little time that I have left
    I'll make this solemn vow,
    To do *some* things I *should* have done
    Not too late, *I'll start right now.*

TO MY DEAR FRIEND
IN SAN FRANCISCO

This morning when I opened my eyes
And saw the sun above
I softly said, "Good morning, Lord,
Bless everyone I love.

Right away I thought of you
And said a loving prayer
That he would bless you specially
And keep you from all care.

I thought of all the happiness
We two have in store
If only it could happen again,
No one deserves it more.

I felt so warm and good inside
My heart was all aglow,
I know God heard my prayer for you, he hears them all,
You know.

If all goes well and it's meant to be
We'll meet again, you wait and see

DEAR LORD

Keep me from bothering the ones I love,
Altho I get lonely for them,
They have their daily work to do,
Don't let me *enter* and bore them.

I'd like to bring joy and gladness
And other good things that gathers
So help me keep my *tears* to myself
But *share* my laughter with others.

DEARHEART: DO YOU KNOW why old folk's

Voices get weaker the older they grow?
Lack of exercise of the vocal chords.
What we don't *use*, we *lose*.

I exercise the body, but not the voice.
Impossible to sing *loud* in church if you
Don't know the words and can't see to read them.

So I've decided (with your permission)
To go out on the porch (when no one is in sight)
And sing as loud and clear, if only
"The scales": fa sol la te do do do do.

So protect me, dear, from those who may say,
"Poor ol' Mayo. gone beyond redemption"
Other words, "nuts."
(Me)
As voice gets stronger,
I'll *shout* the praise.
I hope I may live *here*
The rest of my days.
I like people who die on time.
Don't you?

I HAVE A FRIEND

WHO IS IT WHO MAKES my life easier?
    Who caters to my every need,
    Who does it, oh so *willingly*?
    It's *precious*, Coida, indeed.
    Each day I try to write *something*,
    To ease these *efforts* of mine,
    Perhaps just a silly little poem
    That has no reason or rhyme.
    Some days I may get frantic,
    Might get in your hair,
    Have patience with me, Coida,
    For some day you, too, may be *here*.
    You asked for *something* to remember,
    It won't be just a *ring*,
    The loving *memories* in your heart
    Lasts longer than a *material* thing.
    Soon I will write a happy poem,
    A laugh not a weep,
    The poem I write in the future,
    Will be, I *hope*, one you will *keep*.
    Written in love, May fifteenth, nineteen eighty-nine
                               in my ninety seventh year.

A PIPE DREAM

FROM SAN FRANCISCO TO ALABAMA

This is where I'd like to go
No fire engines pass, no whistles blow
No crowds, no noise, no horrible sound.
I'd have just stillness all around
Not real stillness but just the trees
Swaying in the gentle breeze
And water running over stones
Just soft and gentle natural tones.

If it weren't for sight, sound and smell
I'd like this city very well,
But when I try to get some rest
I like the country lots the best.

I get to thinking, that I must
Just leave the city's dirt and dust
Get out where the air is clear,
I'm goona do it, do you hear?

And I dooed it in nineteen eighty five.

JANUARY 7th 1988

0 0 0 oh, lookie,
"Snow snow, falling snow,
Play with us before you go,

Rain rain, stay away,
Come again some other day.

BLESS THEM

WE, IN OUR WARM BEDS, do not know
   The hazards these dear ones have in this snow,
   So if you don't get the care you expect
   Thank God and be thankful for what you do get.

"IT IS WISE TO STAY out of a fight,
   Only! fools insist on quarreling."
   How stupid to decide before
   Knowing the facts.
   Self-control means controlling
   The tongue.
   "Nothing is ever sliced so thin
   That it doesn't have two sides."

TAKE TIME, DON'T FORGET

I WOKE UP EARLY ONE morning,
    Rushed right into the day,
    I had so much I wanted to do
    That I *forgot* to pray.
    Things got all tight around me
    Everything became a task,
    I wondered, "why doesn't God help me?"
    He answered, "you didn't ask."
    I got up early *this* morning
    Stopped before smarting the day,
    I had so much I wanted to do,
    But I didn't forget to pray.

WHEN I OPENED MY EYES I thought, let me see,
    May fifth is important, but for whom can it be?
    My thoughts went round and stopped on a dot.
    It's either your birthday or either it's not
    Everyone has to have one day a year
    Taking it for granted, this is yours, my dear
    All I can sense is a "bundle of love"
    Sent from me and my "loved one" above.

NO MATTER HOW MUCH I read
    I discover something new.
    One of the tests of a fine book
    Is that while you are reading
    You put it down and start to think.

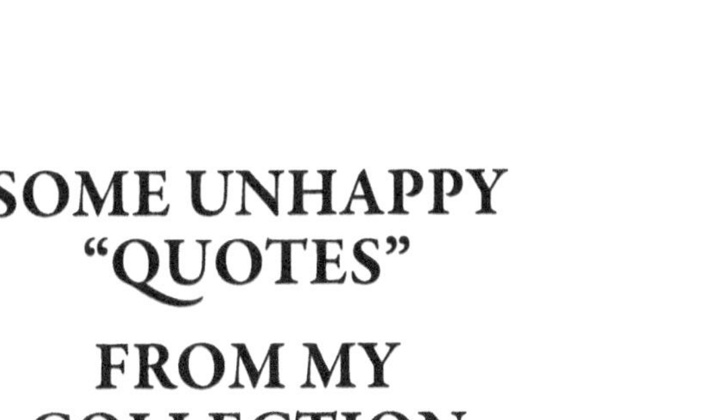

SOME UNHAPPY "QUOTES" FROM MY COLLECTION

EVERY DAY I'M A LITTLE older, if I'm lucky.
None are so old as those who have

Lost enthusiasm.

Bless you for knowing my ears today
Must strain to catch the things you say,
And bless you, too, for seeming to know
My eyes are dim and my wits are slow
I also bless you for making it known
That I'm loved, respected and not alone.

To die is easy, to live is ingenuity.
I've lost my ingenious ? mind.

There's nothing so sad as to remember
"Happy times"

Anyone who has the ability to see beauty
Will never grow old.

              (I see you, "Dearheart.")

Mayo

When it's time to die I don't want to discover
I've never lived.

I'M NOT AFRAID OF TOMORROW,
    I remember yesterday,
    And I have today.
    "Hello," here I am again
    No more moaning, no more pain.
    But I tell you I was sore
    Falling on that bathroom floor.
    I was thinking?
    Oh, forget it.

I AM OUT OF STEP WITH the world.
    The difficulties of life are intended
    To make us *better*, not *bitter*.
    I'll gain respect when people can see
    I'm doing the best I can,
    But there are some who disagree,
    So should I change my plan?
    I'm misunderstood by those of whom
    I have the most respect,
    If only they would *talk* to me,
    Then my faults I would try to correct.
    They finally came and talked to me
    And this they say they find
    That now all things are straightened out
    And was no fault of mine.

So now I'm very happy,
I can't stand being distressed
I'll write my little "nothings" each day
Though silly, I'll do my best.

I TELL THEM

THEY ASK ME WHAT I like about "Summerford"
    They ask if I like the food there,
    I tell them "not only is it the best,"
    But we also set "loving care."

I HAVE A VERY LARGE window
    Can see visitors and flowers outside,
    My room is kept clean and so serene
    I enjoy the dignity and pride.

    What more could I ask in my old age?
    Many are denied such a haven,
    Everyone treats me fine, I can't be unkind
    My home, 'till my next "home" in heaven.

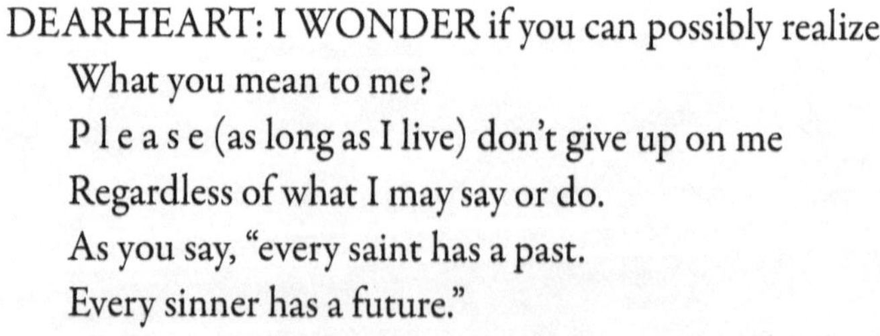

DEARHEART: I WONDER if you can possibly realize
    What you mean to me?
    P l e a s e (as long as I live) don't give up on me
    Regardless of what I may say or do.
    As you say, "every saint has a past.
    Every sinner has a future."
    Do I love you?? Oh, what a question

I'M WRITING THIS ON Sunday,
    Lonely as can be.
    Dearheart, just tell me
    Why you do this to me.
    I won't eat my breakfast,
    Won't go out for fresh air,
    Won't pass the office
    If *you are not there.*
    Forgive all this nonsense,
    Neither rhythm nor rhyme,
    But I do it, Dearheart,
    Just to take up my time.

THE WAY WE LIVE TODAY may leave
    No time for fun.

I TELL YOU, DEARHEART, it's hard to believe
    Of all the kindness I receive
    It's everyday up and down the hall,
    Oh how I love them, I love them all.
    I'm thankful for this, I'm thankful for that
    I'm even thankful for my old hat,
    That shades my eyes from the morning sun,
    And I thank you, Lord, "Thy will be done."

GOD KNOWS OF YOUR LOSS, Irene,
    Understanding will be unfurled,

You know he is in a far better place
Than in this cruel, cruel world.

My love and sympathy,
Mayo

DEARHEART: I READ MY bible at random,

and last night a nurse came in and said,
"I notice you are reading in Micah, my favorite
verse is, Micah, ch.6 verse 8. She has it
written on her cart.

"All God wants me to do is, to be fair
And just and merciful and to walk
Humbly with God."

DEARHEART, ISN'T THAT sweet?
Her name is "Juanita," that's all

AS TOLD TO ME BY A DEAR LITTLE SOUL

DOWN THE HALL (SOUTH)

AS SHE LIES IN HER bed looking so wise,
Her body has failed but not her bright eyes.
She lies there and wonders what they see,
So we wrote a little poem called,
"Look at Me"
What do you see? What do you see?
What are you thinking when you look at me?
A crabby old woman, not very wise
With a shaky habit and far away eyes,
Who dribbles her food and makes *no reply,*
When the nurse, loud and clear,
Says, "I do wish you'd try."
Once she was happy, her husband and she,
Yes, they had children, the number is three.
Now they're all busy rearing their own
She remembers the years of love that she's known
She's now an old woman, the world is cruel
Nature makes old age look like a fool,
She thinks of the years, all too few, gone too fast
But accepts the fact that "nothing can last."

So open your eyes, nurse, open and see
Not a crabby old woman, look closer it's *me*.
She is no longer with us

THE WISDOM OF "DEARHEART"

OVER AND OVER AGAIN
No matter which way I turn,
I always find every day of my life
Some lesson I have to learn.
I listen to "Dearheart," my friend
Her wisdom *must* come from above,
She says, "Don't look for the *end*,
But *live* in this world, with *love*.
So I'll ignore the bad, accept the good,
And live my life the way I should,
Each day I'll do the best I can,
Over and over again.

Dearheart: they say when one door is closed
Another one will open.
I have been looking at the closed door
So long that I forgot the open door

                    Until *now*.

I am working on a book that I will leave to you.

SHIRLEY SMITH

You are never any closer to
Heaven on earth
Than when you are in a
Garden of flowers.

For now the winter is past
The rain is over and gone
The flowers appear in the garden
The time of singing has come.

- from "Song of Solomon"

A little raindrop left the sky
And as it waved its last goodbye
The Lord smiled down from up above
And blessed that raindrop with his love.

That little raindrop danced until
It landed on my windowsill
Into my flower box it came
That precious little drop of rain.

It touched a seed and flowers grew
So bright against a sky of blue
And fragrant blossoms filled the air,
Because God took the time to care.

THINK

Of a little wild flower in the forest
Growing up all alone from the sod,
Budding them blossoms in all its beauty
But no one sees it but God.

TO THE "LEARNED" MEN OF THE WORLD

You can build to the moon, you can tunnel under sod,
But *you* can't *make* a little dandelion
For that "spark of life" comes only from God,
So men, there's no need of your tryin'.

LAST NIGHT THE RAIN came pouring down
It was no little shower,
The lightning flashed the thunder roared
Now *that* is real "God power"
This morning old sol rose over the trees
Smiling so big and bright,
Do you suppose he has any idea
What all that happened last night

JO

Why do you ask the impossible
To be wise and not be a fool.
Do you expect me to remember
Everything I learned in school?

I tackled your task of impossible,
I did my best but I *blew* it,
I was positive, it can't be done"
But you come along and do it.

**2yy u r
2yy u b
I c u r
2yy 4 me**

SOME "QUOTES" FROM MY COLLECTION

The trouble of being a good "sport"

  you have to lose to prove it.

I don't want to be a "has been" or a "will be,"

  I'm an "iser."

Success is how high you bounce after hitting bottom.

Be nice to your friends, if it weren't for them

  you would be a perfect stranger.

A friend is a stranger you haven't met yet.

"Love thy neighbor even if it hurts."

They say age is mind over matter,

  if you don't mind what does it matter?

I can't get old anymore, I am.

Too bad the man who has money to burn,

  can't take it with him.

If you want your ship to come in sooner,

  swim out to meet it.

Whenever you can, hang around the "lucky"

Too many of us would rather stare at a problem

  than to face it.

It isn't hard to make a mountain out of a molehill,

  just add a little "dirt."

God gives the birds their food,

  but he doesn't throw it in their nest.

The thing that is most often opened by mistake,

  is "the *human mouth*."

When you leave footprints in the sands of time,

  don't leave only the mark of a "heel."

October Fourteenth

Bear ones: happy returns of your "great day"
No card, no gift, just a sheet of paper to tell you
I think of you very, very often,
Happy remembrance, "Seeing little Betty walking alone,
Down the aisle, to meet her "Dearheart" at the altar.
Sad remembrance, how hurt my "loved one" was when he asked
You to come see his house, you said you would come after church.
He w a i t e d

You never came.

Friends? All they remember of him is, "He left a mess"

"Congratulations."

Written in love,
Mayo

WE HAVE LITTLE MEETINGS, just we three,
  Lou Seay, Mayo and Gertrude Lee.
We read the bible and other things,
You've no idea the pleasure it brings.
In reading the bible, we don't ascertain
We ask Sandra Abbott to please explain,
She knows her bible, but we are told
We can't take her time, she's on the *payroll.*
This ode is not finished, may have different ends,
But this we know, we're mighty good friends.
The guy who brags that he has a head
On his shoulders, may have a point there
There are two things some people

Never seem to get,
All they want and all they deserve.

WHEN IT'S "SCRUB DAY" for Mayo
In she comes and out she goes
Pure as a lily
And smelling like a rose.
Oh, yea ?

I asked the nurse for a "whirlpool" bath,
We can't, that's for skin disease only,
My arms, legs and back hurt so much
But they said I was pulling a phony.

I asked again but all she said
Was "sorry, we just can't do it.

In the night I thought tomorrow
I'll go to my friend, Ms. Pruitt.
all I ask is a little comfort and care
For which I pay big money,
But all I get from the nursery dear
Is "we just can't do it, honey."
Oh phooey.
I'll bet little Barbara will fix it.

DO WE REALLY KNOW BARBARA PRUETT?

SHE GOES ABOUT DOING good in her quiet way,
    Never expecting praise or gratitude.
    Her "motto" must be "nothing is troublesome
    that we do willingly"

MY ODE TO
BARBARA

WITH ALL THE PRESSURES and duties
    She has to go through every day
    She still takes time to be human,
    And show kindness along the way.

    Today she made someone happy, (me)
    With her thoughtfulness, that's why I say,
    Is it any wonder why we love her?
    We *should* give "thanks" for her every day.

    She is a very unique and precious lady.
    ? Pruett, Pruett, how do you do it?

DOT WRIGHT, YOU ARE TRULY MY FRIEND

Who else could I turn to, were it not for you?
When I'm confused, you know what to do.

You dispersed my holiday sadness and gloom
By inviting me to your little "mom's" home

To meet your family, so beautiful and fine,
And you said, *proudly*, "they're *relatives of mine*."

Dear, Dot; how fortunate can you be?
You'll never be lonely or *alone* like *me*.
mI thank you again, may God above

Bless your dear families,

Written in Love,

Mayo

WHO, ME?

Dot, so you tell me I'm not distressed,
Because I get up and try to get dressed
I see in the mirror, I look sooo forlorned
I'm no raving beauty when unadorned.

FROM "MAYO" TO "DOT"

If this is the way I appear to you,
There's nothing else for me to do.

But wear the "lacies" in my hair,
If others laugh, well, I won't care

I'm not a "teeny" in disguise
I'm wearing them only for *your* eyes

FROM DOT TO MAYO

Once in a while a friend is found
Who proves right from the start
To be the special kind of friend who really warms the heart,
Once in a while a friendship's made that's really lasting, too
And that's the kind of friendship I've known since I met you.

FROM "DOT" TO "MAYO"

In this world where so much seems the same,
Where people try to be like everyone else,
Instead of individuals,
You are special.
When so much is predictable, you are full of surprises
Always saying and doing the Unexpected,
Always refreshingly different.
You are your own unique, one of a kind,
Wonderful person.
Fun, spontaneous, original and absolutely
Marvelous to know

SO LONG "SNOOKS"

You say you are leaving
And it breaks my heart,
But there comes a time
When good friends must part.

There's a time to be silent
There's a time to "inspire"
There's a time to keep working
And a time to "retire."

And since you are leaving
What more can I do?
But say, "God bless"
It was *marvelous* knowing you.

Geraldine, I don't know why,
But I die a little, when I say "good bye."

P.S . Do you know my last name is "Hindle"?

Do you know I am ninety six?
Do you know I'm a kind old soul?

Or do you?
Just "Mayo"

TIME WAS, NOT SO LONG ago that I would say "grace"
But God, I didn't like the food.

I tried, weeks passed, I didn't feel good,
I lost weight.
Then I heard a voice loud and clear, "eat."
I tried and said "grace" in earnest. I felt better
Gained three pounds and ate everything they
Put before me and
"Licked the spoon."
Thank you lady Rowe for helping God
"Make me eat."
Mayo
"Rowe, Rowe, where'd you go?"

It was so lonely while you were gone,

Oh yes, the good eats came on and on,
But even with Dorothy's pretty face
We can't let anyone take your place.

Next year when on vacation you go
If we're still here, we'll let you know
That we love and miss you, Geraldine Rowe
So say "the eaters" and hungry Mayo.

SINCE YOU "INSIST" in leaving,
   Here's hoping you have a healthy, happy,
   Comfortable and easy life, with that "retired fellow"
   You are living with.

   I love you so much, and him too.
   But
   When you leave, *don't* let me know
   Don't say, "good bye," just go go go.

P l e a s e don't check me off your list of friends.

DARLING MARY

A LOVING VOICE AND a gentle touch,
That's why, to me, darling means so much.

You came, we talked, then had a bite,
And while we talked, things seemed so right.
It's sad to think when all is done
We're far apart and no more fun.

If all goes well and it's meant to be
God may let us meet again--we three
Nora and Mayo and silly Mary,
Way down in Florida, in February.

Fanny dear, it's being said
You always want to be ahead,
Quoting the ways and means and such,
Don't you think that's a little too much?

Come back here and you will find
It's much more comfortable being behind,
No one cares what we do or say

So they can't criticize us that way.
So take it easy, fanny, and don't fuss,

Come back here, be one of us.

The Lowbrows

or

What is it Fanny, that you want?
Always wanting to be out front,
Unless you change your life style soon
You'll find yourself on the way to the moon.
We won't tolerate your gift of gab.
Going on and on, that's all we've had.
Only one thing more we can tell
"We can get along without you very well"

EGO

Some days I am very proud,
Think things are just fine.
I worked *hard* for what I have
And they are really *mine*!

I am a self-made man, think only of tomorrow,
I didn't give a helping hand
For I *neither lend* nor *borrow*.
One day I picked up a *bible*.
Found I could get "help" in my fight.
So I breathed out ego, breathed *in God*.
It turns out, "the bible is right."

TRUST AND OBEY

When you feel lousy and out of sorts

And wish that you were dead,
Just grab that phone call two four 0
And talk to "Doctor Fred"

He'll say,
"Take two aspirin and go to bed
Call me in the morning"
So you listen to what he said
And heed his words of warning.

So I took two pills and went to bed,
Next morning I felt *great*

That's 'cause I listened to what "Fred said"
So do it 'fore it's "too late."

Without "loved ones" like you there would be no me,
What you give with your heart, is more than under the tree

So help me, dear Lord, to love them more,
Than I've ever loved before,
When I'm lonely and when I pray
Help me bless them every day.

Wilma, Wilma, on the go

Ever faster, never slow

Like a race horse in the bridle

Busy hands, never idle

Sit and watch her for a while, her redeeming feature is her
Smile busy, busy helping "the needy"

Guess we'll have to call her, "speedy."

"Show me a man" this day and age
Who's mind is not on money,
I know of such a man to day,

I'll tell you about him, honey.

This man is busy from morning till night
And it's not on just a "hobby."
He works to help the aged and sick,
I'll tell you his name, it's "Bobby."

FORGIVE

Dear little Robinson girl, I say from the start,
You have a kind and generous heart.
You're so full of business and I guess
In your position, you think it best.

Be more like a pussy cat or turtle dove,
Don't make it so difficult for us to love
And don't be so distant, we all can see
You demand respect, even from me.

You're a little too feisty, now this is the end.
I love you, little girl and want to be your friend.
Forgive this nonsensical outburst from me,
It's the way I am, not what I want to be.

Me ? Not me. I don't know.
who.

Yes, I know.
It's just that old lovable Mayo?

TO WHOM IT MAY CONCERN

If I only I had a larger room
How happy I would be
A desk for my typewriter
And I could turn on my own TV.

Put someone in the other bed
With a heart not made of stone.
I'd like to help take care of her
And I wouldn't feel alone.

I won't mention this again
It's all up to you;
But *if* I had a larger room
I could do what I like to do.

RESTLESSNESS

It seems I've always been active,
Now I find it hard to just recline,
So I look for some task or purpose
That merits these *efforts* of mine.

This search may grow rather frantic
And I might get in your hair,
Be patient and try to see my side,
For one day, you too, may be there.

I won't bother you again 'till next time

BUT AIN'T IT THE TRUTH?

(Copied) author unknown
(Last four lines by Mayo)
According to the experts
The country's in a mess,
But just how bad it's going to be
Is anybody's guess.

Unemployment's on the rise
Inflation's here to stay
The economic downfall
Is just a step away.

Our democratic system
Is going down the drain,
The good old days are over
And will never come again.

And as we read and listen
To those prophecies of doom
We sink a little deeper
Into hopelessness and gloom.

But let's stop shaking in our boots
And prove to one and all

We're not licked yet, and you can bet
We'll rise above it all.

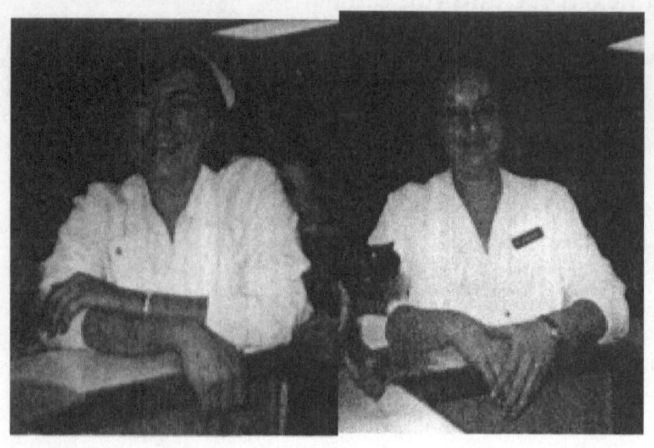

WE'RE ALL SO THANKFUL for little nurse, Trudi,
   Who does many things, beyond the "call of duty"
   And precious Vicki, when my breakfast she brings,
   Never forgets the little things,
   like sugar, straws, etc.
   So you see, Lord, why our days start so bright,
   It's cause these two "gals" do everything right.

SPOTLESS

ODE TO THE LADIES WEARING shirts of blue,
    We, in our wheelchairs, keep watching you,
    Pushing that old bucket with that mop
    Brooms and dustpans, seems you never stop.
    Running that "shiner" down the hall the full length,
    We often wonder where you get your strength.
    But this we do know, you can take our word,
    There's no sweeter "home" than "The Summerford"
    Bless you dear ladies, we seal with a kiss.
    We're fortunate to be living in a clean home like this.
        Every time I see you bend over,
          it hurts my back

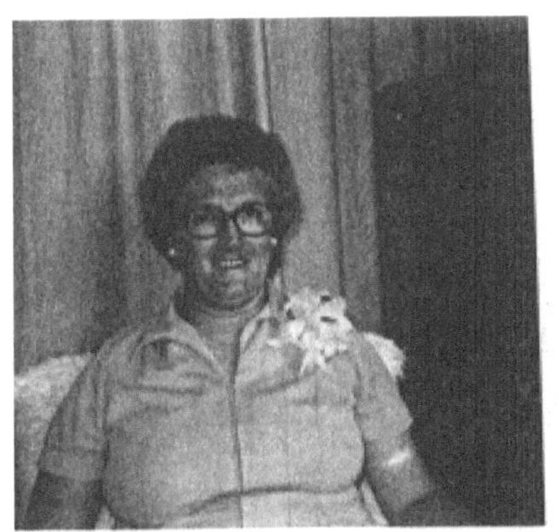

WHY?

Why are they *letting* you leave, Lucille?
When we need you so much,
Who can we tell our troubles to
When we're lonely, bored and such?
The "workers" are all too busy
Doing the *basic* needs
To listen to our woe's and hurts
Or to our whining pleas.
We lie in bed and wonder why
Life throws us such a deal,
We need a word of encouragement,
That only *you* can give, Lucille.
So we'll take what comes, good or bad
Putting in our time each day,
Oh, what a time to be leaving, Lucille,
We'll ask God, *why*, when we pray.
Love goes with you from all *of us*

and Mayo, tu

THREE BONES ARE NECESSARY for a good life
-1- Wish bone
-2- Back bone
-3- Funny bone

STAY IN THERE

WHEN THINGS GO WRONG you heave a sigh,
   The *funds* are low and the *bills* are high
   If pressure gets you down a bit
   Keep right on going, don't you quit.
   Life is *rough* and you must learn
   To stay in line and take your turn,
   Sooner or later if you go slow
   You may succeed with that *one more blow*.
   You'll reach your goal by *not* giving up
   Someday you'll win that "platinum" cup.
   Success is failure inside out,
   Never listen to a word of doubt,
   You're getting closer to that "hit"
   Stay in there, honey, *don't you quit*.

Last Friday, when you called me
(in case you forgot)
I told you I was on the throne,
(in other words, "the pot")
I also said I was weary, you said
"You will find"
That most of that weariness is
Just the state of mind.
I realized how true it is and
Decided to *fight back*
Do you know where that fight got me?
Right back in the sack.

   So.....

Back in the sack, back in the sack
That's
Where
I am
now,
back in the sack.
Goodnight

DREAM... THE WORLD is so fair
    Dream... and not have a care
    Dream... and you'll find
    Sure enough, it's all in the mind.
    Wake up and live.

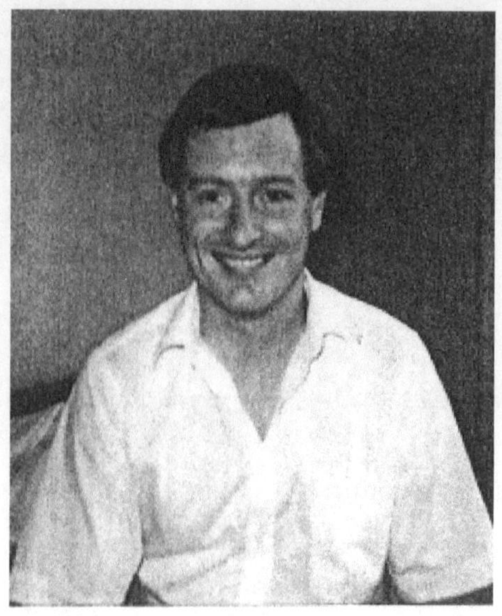

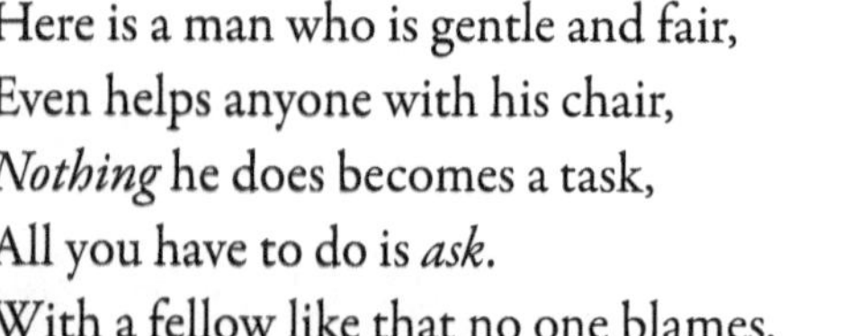

Here is a man who is gentle and fair,
Even helps anyone with his chair,
Nothing he does becomes a task,
All you have to do is *ask*.
With a fellow like that no one blames,
He's always so *willing*, his name is "James"

THE CLASS OF THE EIGHTIES & NINETIES

We're not much to look at
With our arms up in the air,
Doing our daily exercise
While sitting in our chair.

But Jana says, "Chop wood"
Do it ten times or more.
Now, don't you feel better?
No, our bones are sore.

But we *will not* give up
We'll keep trying as we should,
'Cause Jana says, "That's just fine"
We'd do better if we *could.*

"The future champs"??
Jana, coach.

CHRISTMAS, NINETEEN EIGHTY SEVEN

WHO DO I THINK OF WHEN I sit down to rest?
  Who is that dear one, who gives the best?
  Oh, it's so comfortable when I recline,
  And just to think, it's really mine.
  Each day I cover it with a "throw"
  To return it clean, when it's time to go.
  It may be years, or maybe tomorrow,
  Whenever the time, there'll be no sorrow.
  I thank you, dear Sandra, I love you so much.
  You've made my Christmas with your loving touch
  I'll "recline" now and "decline" later.
  Much
  Later
  I hope.

NO EARTHLY GIFT, BUT one from above,
  Straight from my heart, "A bundle of love."

THERE'S NO DOUBT
ABOUT IT.

SEE WHAT I MEAN SANDRA, when I say
God guides and keeps us safe every day.
The day we went shopping, we didn't know
The very next day, there'd be ten inches of snow

See, God is so good, keeps us safe and secure
I am so glad he answered my prayer.

MY SANDRA, MY SANDRA

OH HOW I NEED YOU

ENCOURAGEMENT IS WHAT I need
    When I'm lonely and spirits are low
    I thank God for my really true friend
    To whom, I know, I can go.

    Just a word or a pat on the back
    Is all a lonely heart needs,
    So I'll hold up my chin, let love come in
    And thank *you* for hearing my pleas.

    Dear:
    If I get confused and feel so alone
    And don't know what to do
    And if I'm left with only one friend
    I hope that one will be you.

A SPECIAL GIFT FOR JULIE

Over and over again,
No matter which way you turn,
You'll always find every day of your life
Some lesson you have to learn.

Listen to your parents, who are wise,
Wisdom comes from above.
Don't strive to *acquire*, strive to *become*
And live in this world with love.

So *ignore* the bad, accept the *good*
And live your life the way you should.
You, *Julie*, will say, *"Life is good."*
Over and over again.
Mayo 96 (1988)

Written in love
Especially for .
Julie Paige
(my new friend)

A beautiful young lady, now only ten,
Comes to see me now and then,
Always comes with a great big smile,
Now *that* is what makes life worthwhile.

She's getting an education, staying in school
Better "young and wise" than "old and a fool"
As long as I live I'll love her truly,
And Jesus loves you, too, little Julie.

Written in love especially for Julie S. (my new friend).

ATTENTION, ALL
TEENAGERS

Tell the truth, pay your debts
And learn to say "no"
With a "motto" like that
You are bound to grow.

This old world is very cruel,
Get an education, finish your school.
Follow your "motto," your days will glow
If you tell the truth, pay your debts
and learn to say "no."

Memorize it and say it slow,
Tell the truth, pay your debts
And learn to say "no"

"MAYO"

I'm not looking for the *sunset*
When my work on earth is done,
I am looking o'er the mountains
To see the *rising sun*.

I am looking up, not downward
When I set my earthly *goal*,
It will be high on a mountain
Where this world can take "no toll."

I will look up to the heavens
See that beautiful "home" on high.
That is where I am going
when it's time to say, "good bye."

Mayo is a cheerful old soul, isn't she?
Does she really believe she will
Go to heaven?
"Yes," positively.

MY PHILOSOPHY

AS YEARS FLY BY I AM giving more time thinking of what we owe the young ones.

I don't mean financial or social nor family affairs, but we should be more like a "peach" inside while becoming like a "prune" outside.

An old person who gets all dried up, brittled and wrinkled and full of complaints is a total "drag"

Most people allow age to do awful things to them.

We should get mellower and more tolerant and wiser to compensate for our external countenance.

Instead, most people let themselves

become disapproving and self-centered and even more constipated.

Young people have a natural love for oldsters who have kept the spirit of youth.

They reject and resent the old ones who have forgotten what it is like to be young.

It is the inner spirit that the youngsters respond to, not the surface appearance.

An old person who tries to look, act and dress like a junior, is simply an object of pity.

One, who feels left out by the young, tends to blame it on "changing times" when it's really their unwillingness to broaden their understanding and sympathies.

Most of us get worse as we get older when we should get better.

We settle into our own little deformation instead of coming out of our "hard shell" and meeting the new world, at least, "halfway."

   1987 Mayo

95 yrs.

AN ODE TO AGNES, ONE OF GOD'S ANGELS

WHEN SHE MISSES WE say, "Sakes alive"
    What's happened to our little five by five?
    She's some place she should,
    Going about doing good,
    Without her we feel we can't thrive.
    We must have patience and wait,
    She comes but sometimes she's late,
    So we can't sit and fuss
    And tell her she must,
    She might leave us to our fate.
    She walks these long halls the full length,
    The one she works *for*, gives her strength,
    Goes from room to room

Dispersing their gloom.
Giving them courage and faith.
We need her the rest of our days,
It helps us *so much when she prays.*
So God hear my plea
Keep sending her to me,
I'll give you the glory and praise.
Written in love, Mayo

HELLO

This is not a "Dear John" letter of long ago,
When your "gal" loved another, and *told you so*.

But from a huzzy, who still has fun
Telling the world how it should be run.

To avoid the bad and accept the good
And love each other as we should.

Now, about that date? "If", ten years ago?
Why, dear heart, were you so slow?
So the year two thousand, we'll make a date
I do hope Dear John, it won't

    be
    too
    late.

Ninety five plus, now let me see
one hundred and eight, that's how old I'll be.
Do you think that's too long to wait for me ???

    (((OK punk, I don't like you either)))

IF HALF THE WORLD DOESN'T know what the other half is doing, it's nice to know that half the people mind their own business.
6/9/87

DO WE THANK HER?

WE SEE YOU, JO ANN, coming down the hall,
    Bringing clean clothes for us all.
    They go "in" shabby, dirty and *phew*
    You bring them back, looking like new.
    For your kindness and the way you serve,
    Do you get "thanks" for what you deserve?
    I'll thank you, Joann for all the rest,
    I pray for your strength and for you, *dear, the best*.

                    Mayo

"written in love"

PLEASANT SURPRISE

THEY TELL ME I'M GOING to have a visitor,
    None other than honorable Judge Greene,
    Coming to visit an old lady
    Whom he has never seen.

    I hope you won't be disappointed
    From things you have been told,
    Sometimes I'm a wee bit pesky
    Other times somewhat bold.

    True, we may never meet again
    Old "time" is fast aflying,
    Perhaps the ones you meet today
    Tomorrow will be dying.

    Written in respect.

Mayo
I'm expecting? (you)

    I live each day as though
    I expect to live forever.

JUST A BIG PAIN AND a hurt,
    The body is failing, is the mind still alert?

MY MOTTO: BE KIND, be gentle
    Dependent Mayo loves you.

THE FINALE

When I close this book forever
And it's handed over to you
I hope you will remember
Some things I tried to do.

I love life and all its blessings
Try to live in peace and love,
I pray to our heavenly father
To take me to his "home" above.

I'll write my epitaph before cremation
To write it is a "must"
To all my friends and loved ones
Simply, "Please, excuse my dust."

A LONG TIME AGO

'TWAS A WEEK AFTER CHRISTMAS, I was feeling fine,
The date of that day was December twenty nine.
I went to sleep and woke up with joy,
Heaven had sent us an eleven pound boy.

Now he's a man, Lord give him health,
Love and confidence, not necessarily wealth.
Guide him and keep him safe every day,
I love him, I miss him, *he's so far away.*

Dear God, I'm his mother,
Don't leave me alone, please take my hand when it's time to "go home."

But don't hurry, God, I'm only eighty.
written in 1972.

MY SON

I TOOK A PIECE OF *living* clay,
 And gently formed it day by day,
 And molded it with *power* and *art*
 A young boy's soft and receiving heart.

 I came again. when years were gone,
 It was a man I looked upon,
 He still that early molding bore.
 But I can change that form no more.

Photo by Jude Johnston

MY SON, MY SON.

Dear God, you have taken my "loved one"
And left me here all alone.
I'll work and try to be worthy,
But this world is no longer my home.
I'll pray for strength and be thankful,
Each morning when I see the sun rise,
I'll wait, dear God, for your invitation
To come home to you in the skies.

BLESS ALL YOU, DEAR ones, who have shared my grief.
　　sad date.... April seventh, nineteen eighty seven.
　　He washed my eyes with tears
　　That I might see,
　　The reason he took my son
　　away from me.

OBITUARY

On the Death of Will Hindle
Mentor and Friend

BRUCE POSNER EMAILED two weeks ago to tell me that Will Hindle had died in his doctor's parking lot, apparently of a heart attack, back in April. It had taken more than two months for word to reach from Alabama to Chicago, a sad testament to the dearth of communication in the independent film community today. For Will Hindle was one of our very greatest film artists, and the loss of this master's wit and fluid sense of beauty is a tragedy for us all.

Ordinarily, I respond to the death of others as an inevitability, almost as a relief to our too-crowded planet and culture, and am rarely shocked. But I am shocked at the death of Hindle. I feel his death as a great personal loss, and an irremediable loss to our film culture. Will Hindle left behind a substantial body of work, including at toast three masterpieces (*Watersmith, Chinese Firedrill,* and *Pasteur 3*). But it is painfully clear, at least to me, that his work as an artist was unfinished when he died. The films he dreamed of making in the studio, he labored years to build in the backwoods of Alabama will never be made. His heart gave out many years before his mind, his wit or his imagination would have faltered. Witness *Trekkerriff,* likely to be Hindle's last film, shown here in silent version in 1984, manifesting even in its unfinished state, Hindle's acute commentary on the state of modem humanity, but to which has been added a new depth of subtlety indicative of the work of a fully mature master.

And this is why I am shocked and saddened by Will Hindle's death. He was not a young man (he must have been near sixty, though he always refused to tell his age), and his passing not inexplicable like that of Mozart, or Schubert... or Jean Vigo. Rather it is the shock of losing a *master* who was, after decades of adversity, of struggle against demons within and without, on the verge of producing his final and greatest work. I have been cheated, as have all who loved Hindle's work, by a more-than-usually unkind fate. More than usually, death has triumphed, and as I try to find some sense, some good in this tragedy, try as I may, I cannot. I can only fall on my religious convictions (that "mixture of sense and nonsense," as James Broughton would say) and assume that Will Hindle lives on in a better world than the one he left. God knows. Hindle was not suited for this one.-

John Luther Schofill

July 12, 1987

AFTERWORD

TO MY DEAREST MOTHER....

Again, as in most of recent years, I cannot find a card to say anything near the affection I feel for you. Indeed, I doubt if I will ever again rely on a ready-made card. If I want to send the very best I don't think I would rely on Hallmark... because you're better than Hallmark ever thought of.

I can't bring myself to "apologize" for my shortcomings in your eyes (and in my own) this past year. Rather, I would simply pray and hope that you be wise enough and strong enough to come out of it all smelling like roses and smiling and forgiving (not to mention smarter).

It's kind of tough on my system not being able to lift you above all care, not being able to cradle you in, not luxury, but in comfort... the kind of comfort that would screen out unnecessary cruelties from unthinking ones, the kind of comfort that would give you time to read, to think broader and better thoughts, the kind of comfort which would allow you to be more fully the good woman you are. It is painful to me not to be able to help you.

Perhaps yet, life has in store for us both some sweet and unexpected surprise of fulfillment. Admittedly, it does seem as though "things" will never turn out. But with a little push here and there, it just may be that chances will be better than 50-50 that we may yet see our best happinesses. Most of the happinesses in life occur solely in the head... and we've still got ours, so we still have a very good chance.

Never, never doubt my deep and abiding affection and love for you. If you start out the year in no other way, start it knowing that this will never, can never change.

Love, Willie

About the Author

Mayo Hindle, who resided in the deep South, wrote most of her poetry as she approached 100 years of age. She was beloved by many people, including those in Summerford, a Nursing Home, where she lived her final years. She was especially beloved by her son, a well-known experimental film maker, Will Hindle. These poems are a testament to Mayo's wisdom, creativty, and beauty as a person.

Read more at https://www.allroneofus.com/.